HELLO EVERYBODY,

WELCOME ABOARD MY POETRY TRAIN! HAVE YOU ALL GOT YOUR TICKETS? GOOD. I'VE JUST BEEN INTO THE STATION BUFFET TO SEE IF THERE WERE ANY MORE PASSENGERS AND THE PLACE IS FULL OF HAIRY SAVAGES EATING EVERYTHING IN SIGHT. SO I THINK WE'LL LEAVE THEM BEHIND, DON'T YOU?

ON OUR JOURNEY YOU'LL SEE ALL SORTS OF THINGS; COWS AND SHEEP, OWLS, A WITCH AND, IN THE DARK WOOD, THE DARKLING ELVES. WATCH OUT FOR THEM! IF YOU WANT TO *SOUND* LIKE A TRAIN, READ THE ENGINE DRIVER POEM, ON PAGE 14, OUT LOUD. INFACT, ITS MORE FUN IF YOU READ ALL THE POEMS OUT LOUD.

VERY SOON WE'LL BE AT THE SEASIDE AND WE CAN SWIM OR PADDLE. OH, WE'LL HAVE A LOVELY TIME, SO WE'D BETTER GET GOING.

TOOT! TOOT! *Bernard Cribbins*

ALONG THE LINE

with
Bernard Cribbins

Illustrated by Annabel Spenceley
Edited by Jenny Wood

Macdonald

1 In the Buffet

Sky in the pie!

Waiter, there's a sky in my pie
Remove it at once if you please
You can keep your incredible sunsets
I ordered mincemeat and cheese

I can't stand nightingales singing
Or clouds all burnished with gold
The whispering breeze is disturbing the peas
And making my chips go all cold

I don't care if the chef is an artist
Whose canvases hang in the Tate
I want two veg. and puff pastry
Not the Universe heaped on my plate

OK I'll try just a spoonful
I suppose I've got nothing to lose
Mm . . .the colours quite tickle the palette
With a blend of delicate hues

6

The sun has a custardy flavour
And the clouds are as light as air
And the wind a chewier texture
(With a hint of cinnamon there?)

This sky is simply delicious
Why haven't I tried it before?
I can chew my way through to Eternity
And still have room left for more

Having acquired a taste for the Cosmos
I'll polish this sunset off soon
I can't wait to tuck into the night sky
Waiter! Please bring me the Moon!

ROGER MCGOUGH

7

Yellow butter

Yellow butter purple jelly red jam black bread

Spread it thick
Say it quick

Yellow butter purple jelly red jam black bread

Spread it thicker
Say it quicker

Yellow butter purple jelly red jam black bread

Now repeat it
While you eat it

Yellow butter purple jelly red jam black bread

Don't talk
With your mouth full!

MARY ANN HOBERMAN

8

A thousand hairy savages

A thousand hairy savages
Sitting down to lunch
Gobble gobble glup glup
Munch munch munch.

SPIKE MILLIGAN

WHO'S HAD MY BEANS ON TOAST?

Through the teeth

Through the teeth
And past the gums.
Look out, stomach,
Here it comes!

ANON

I eat my peas with honey

I eat my peas with honey,
I've done it all my life,
It makes the peas taste funny,
But it keeps them on my knife.

ANON

9

2 On the Platform

There was a young farmer of Leeds

There was a young farmer of Leeds
Who swallowed six packets of seeds,
It soon came to pass
He was covered with grass,
And he couldn't sit down for the weeds.

ANON

Herbaceous Plodd

Herbaceous Plodd
is rather odd.
His eyes are red,
his nose is blue,
his neck and head
are joined by glue.
He only dines
on unripe peas,
bacon rinds
and melted cheese.
He rarely talks,
he never smiles,
but goes for walks
with crocodiles.

MICHAEL DUGAN

Maggie

There was a small maiden named Maggie,
Whose dog was enormous and shaggy;
The front end of him
Looked vicious and grim –
But the tail end was friendly and waggy.

ANON

Imogen Claire

Imogen Claire
hasn't a care,
she will not brush
or comb her hair,
or wash her face,
or blow her nose,
but we suppose
that as she grows
she will
get
better.

GEORGIE ADAMS

Herbert Breeze

Herbert Breeze
Had three exploding knees.
One he kept as a spare,
The other two he wore everywhere.

STEPHEN SCHEDING

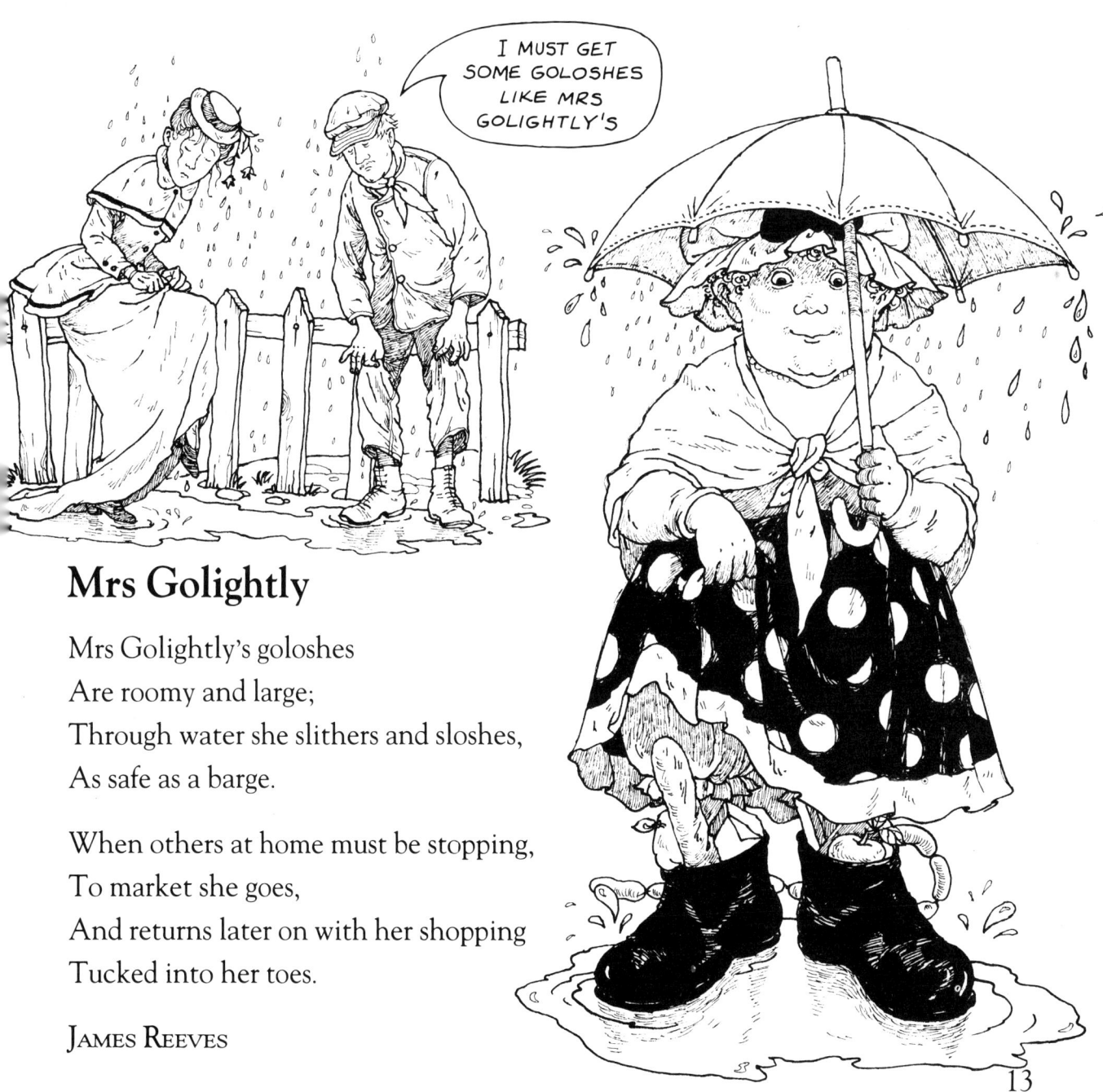

Mrs Golightly

Mrs Golightly's goloshes
Are roomy and large;
Through water she slithers and sloshes,
As safe as a barge.

When others at home must be stopping,
To market she goes,
And returns later on with her shopping
Tucked into her toes.

JAMES REEVES

13

3 Along the Line

The Engine Driver

The train goes running along the line,
Jicketty-can, jicketty-can.
I wish it were mine, I wish it were mine,
Jicketty-can, jicketty-can.
The Engine Driver stands in front –
He makes it run, he makes it shunt.

Out of the town,
Out of the town,
Over the hill,
Over the down,
Under the bridges,
Across the lea,
Over the ridges
And down to the sea,

With a jicketty-can, jicketty-can,
Jicketty-jicketty-jicketty-can,
Jicketty-can, jicketty-can . . .

CLIVE SANSOM

14

Looe

Bidderly-do, bidderly-do,
I'm on a train and I'm off to Looe.
Ra-ta-ta-tar, ra-ta-ta-tar,
I'm going to visit my Grandmamma.
Tickety-tack, tickety-tack,
Into a tunnel that's ever so black.
A-rumpety-tum, a-rumpety-tum,
I'm taking a present to Granny from Mum.
Tickety-boo, tickety-boo,
I always enjoy the journey to Looe.
Chi-chi-chi-choo,
Chi-chi-chi...........CHOO!

ROLAND EGAN

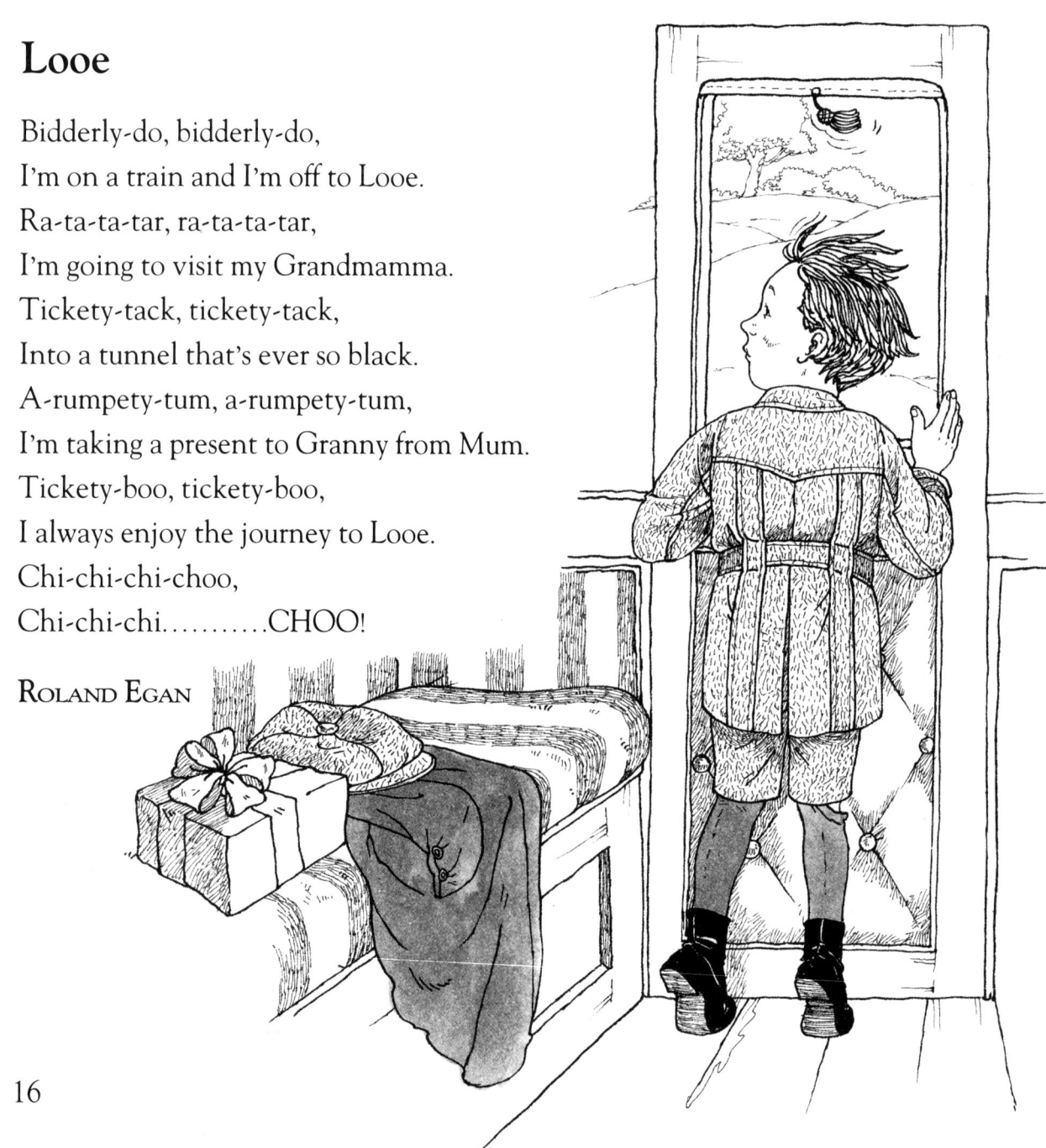

16

Piggy on the railway

Piggy on the railway
Picking up stones,
Along came an engine
And broke Piggy's bones.

"Oy!" said Piggy,
"That's not fair."
"Pooh," said the engine driver,
"I don't care."

Anon

A peanut

A peanut sat on the railroad track,
His heart was all a-flutter.
Along came a train, the 10.15 –
Toot-toot! peanut butter!

Anon

There was a young lady from Spain

There was a young lady from Spain
Who was dreadfully sick on a train,
Not once – but again
and again and again
and again and again and again.

Anon

17

The song the train sang

Now
When the
Steam hisses;
Now when the
Coupling clashes;
Now
When the
Wind rushes,
Comes the slow but sudden swaying,
Every truck and carriage trying
For a smooth and better rhythm,
For a smooth and singing rhythm.

This...is...the...one...
That...is...the...one...
This is the one,
That is the one,
This is the one, that is the one,
This is the one, that is the one.

Over the river, past the mill,
Through the tunnel under the hill;
Round the corner, past the wall,
Through the wood where trees grow tall,
Then in sight of the town by the river,
Brake by the crossing where white leaves quiver.
Slow as the streets of the town slide past
As the windows stare at the jerking of the coaches
Coming into the station approaches.

Stop at the front.
Stop at the front.
Stop . . .at the front.
Stop . . .at the . . .
Stop.

Ahhhh!

NEIL ADAMS

4 Through the Meadows

The moo-cow-moo

The moo-cow-moo has a tail like rope,
An' it's ravelled down where it grows,
An' it's jest like feelin' a piece of soap
All over the moo-cow's nose.

The moo-cow-moo has lots of fun
Jest swingin' its tail about,
But ef he opens his mouth, I run,
Cause that's where the moo comes out.

Edmund Vance Cook

Hurt no living thing

Hurt no living thing;
Ladybird, nor butterfly,
Nor moth with dusty wing,
Nor cricket chirping cheerily,
Nor grasshopper so light of leap,
Nor dancing gnat, nor beetle fat,
Nor harmless worms that creep.

CHRISTINA ROSSETTI

Owl

A wise old owl sat in an oak,
The more he heard the less he spoke;
The less he spoke the more he heard.
Why aren't we all like that wise old bird?

ANON

From a railway carriage

Faster than fairies, faster than witches,
Bridges and houses, hedges and ditches;
And charging along like troops in a battle,
All through the meadows the horses and cattle:
All of the sights of the hill and the plain
Fly as thick as driving rain;
And ever again, in the wink of an eye,
Painted stations whistle by.

Here is a child who clambers and scrambles,
All by himself and gathering brambles;
Here is a tramp who stands and gazes;
And there is the green for stringing the daisies!
Here is a cart run away in the road
Lumping along with man and load;
And here is a mill and there is a river.
Each a glimpse and gone for ever!

ROBERT LOUIS STEVENSON

Who's that bleating?

Who's that bleating
Down by the river?
Sheep are sweating,
Soon they'll shiver.
Back to the farm
Without their wool,
We'll go warm
And they'll go cool.

ELEANOR FARJEON

23

5 In the Dark Wood

The witch

I saw her plucking cowslips,
And marked her where she stood:
She never knew I watched her
While hiding in the wood.

Her skirt was brightest crimson,
And black her steeple hat,
Her broomstick lay beside her –
I'm positive of that.

Her chin was sharp and pointed,
Her eyes were – I don't know –
For when she turned towards me –
I thought it best – to go!

PERCY ILLOT

COULD I SEE YOUR TICKETS PLEASE?

24

The darkling elves

In wildest woods, on treetop shelves,
sit evil beings with evil selves –
they are the dreaded darkling elves
    and they are always hungry.

In garish garb of capes and hoods,
they wait and watch within their woods
to peel your flesh and steal your goods
    for they are always hungry.

Through brightest days and darkest nights
these terrifying tiny sprites
await to strike and take their bites
    for they are always hungry.

Watch every leaf of every tree,
for once they pounce you cannot flee –
their teeth are sharp as sharp can be …
    and they are always hungry.

JACK PRELUTSKY

25

Beware, my child

Beware, my child,
of the snaggle-toothed beast.
He sleeps till noon,
then makes his feast
on chocolate bars
and cakes of yeast
and anyone around-o.

So when you see him,
sneeze three times
and say three loud
and senseless rhymes
and give him all your
saved-up dimes,
or else you'll ne'er be found-o.

SHEL SILVERSTEIN

A room bewitched

In the dark, dark wood, there was a dark, dark house,
And in that dark, dark house, there was a dark, dark room,
And in that dark, dark room, there was a dark, dark cupboard,
And in that dark, dark cupboard, there was a dark, dark shelf,
And on that dark, dark shelf, there was a dark, dark box,
And in that dark, dark box, there was a . . .

GHOST!

ANON

The Witch! The Witch!

The Witch! The Witch! don't let her get you!
Or your Aunt wouldn't know you the next time she met you!

ELEANOR FARJEON

6 At the Seaside

The lobsters and the fiddler crab

The lobsters came ashore one night
In the merry month of June,
And coaxed the fiddler crab to play
A rollicking tango tune.

The lobsters danced, the fiddler played
Till morning, rosy red,
Chased the dancers into the sea
And the fiddler home to bed!

FREDERICK J. FORSTER

O my!

He rocked the boat,
Did Ezra Shank;
These bubbles mark

Where Ezra sank.

ANON

Wonders

Behold the wonders of the mighty deep,
Where crabs and lobsters learn to creep,
And little fishes learn to swim,
And clumsy sailors tumble in.

ANON

Mine

I made a sand castle.
In rolled the sea.
    "All sand castles
      belong to me –
      to me,"
said the sea.

I dug sand tunnels.
In flowed the sea.
    "All sand tunnels
      belong to me –
      to me,"
said the sea.

I saw my pail floating free.
I ran and snatched it from the sea.
    "My sand pail
      belongs to me –
      to ME!"

LILIAN MOORE

There are big waves

There are big waves and little waves,
Green waves and blue,
Waves you can jump over,
Waves you dive through.

Waves that rise up
Like a great water wall,
Waves that swell softly
And don't break at all.

Waves that can whisper,
Waves that can roar,
And tiny waves that run at you
Running on the shore.

ELEANOR FARJEON

First dip

Wave after wavelet goes
Coldly over your toes
And sinks down into the stones.
Another mounts to your knees,
Icy, as if to freeze
Flesh and marrow and bones.
And now another, a higher,
Yellow with foam, and dire
With weed from yesterday's storm.
With a gasp you greet it –
Your shoulders stoop to meet it –
And you find . . . you find . . .
Ah-h-h-h!
You find that the water is warm.

John Walsh

The Slitheree-dee

The Slitheree-dee has crawled out of the sea.
He may catch all the others, but he won't catch me.
No you won't catch me, old Slitheree-dee,
You may catch all the others, but you wo . . .

SHEL SILVERSTEIN

The guppy

Whales have calves,
Cats have kittens,
Bears have cubs,
Bats have bittens;
Swans have cygnets,
Seals have puppies,
But guppies just have little guppies.

OGDEN NASH

33

7 Going Home

Time to go home!
Says the great steeple clock.
Time to go home!
Says the gold weathercock.
Down sinks the sun
In the valley to sleep;
Lost are the orchards
In blue shadows deep.
Soft falls the dew
On cornfield and grass;
Through the dark trees
The evening airs pass:
Time to go home,
They murmur and say!
Birds to their homes
Have all flown away.
Nothing shines now
But the gold weathercock.
Time to go home!
Says the great steeple clock.

JAMES REEVES

Index of Poets

Index of First Lines

The lobsters came ashore one night 28
The moo-cow-moo has a tail like rope 20
The Slitheree-dee has crawled out of the sea 33
The train goes running along the line 14
The Witch! The Witch! don't let her get you! 27
There are big waves and little waves 31
There was a small maiden named Maggie 11
There was a young farmer of Leeds 10
There was a young lady from Spain 17
Through the teeth 9
Time to go home! 34

Waiter, there's a sky in my pie 6
Wave after wavelet goes 32
Whales have calves 33
Who's that bleating? 23

Yellow butter purple jelly red jam black bread 8